THE MANNINGS
Football's Famous Family

by J.A. Worthington

Reading Consultant:
Timothy Rasinski, Ph.D.
Professor of Reading Education
Kent State University

Content Consultant:
Saleem Choudhry
Pro Football Hall of Fame

Red Brick™ Learning

Published by Red Brick™ Learning
7825 Telegraph Road, Bloomington, Minnesota 55438
http://www.redbricklearning.com

Library of Congress Cataloging-in-Publication Data
Worthington, Joe, 1954–
   The Mannings: football's famous family / by Joe Worthington.
   p. cm.—(High five reading)
Includes bibliographical references and index.
   ISBN 0-7368-5741-9 (soft cover)—ISBN 0-7368-5731-1 (hard cover)
   1. Manning, Archie, 1949—Juvenile literature. 2. Manning,
Peyton—Juvenile literature. 3. Manning, Eli, 1981—Juvenile literature.
4. Football players—United States—Biography—Juvenile literature.
5. Fathers and sons—United States—Biography—Juvenile literature.
I. Title. II. Series.
GV939.A1W67 2000
796.332'092'2—dc22

                          2005010094

Created by Kent Publishing Services, Inc.
Designed by Signature Design Group, Inc.
Edited by Jerry Ruff, Managing Editor, Red Brick™ Learning
Red Brick™ Learning Editorial Director: Mary Lindeen

This publisher has made every effort to trace ownership of all copyrighted
material and to secure necessary permissions. In the event of any questions
arising as to the use of any material, the publisher, while expressing regret for
any inadvertent error, will be happy to make necessary corrections.

Photo Credits:
Cover, pages 23, 27, Icon Sports Media/SMI; page 4, Brian Spurlock–U.S.
Presswire/Zuma Press; page 7, Michael Conroy, Associated Press; page 9, A/P
Photo/University of Tennessee; page 11, Mark Humphrey, Associated Press; page
13, John Dunn, Zuma Press; pages 14, 21, 30, Associated Press, A/P; page 17,
Focus On Sport/Getty Images; page 18, Getty Images; page 24, Bruce Newman,
Associated Press; page 29, Bill Kostroun, Associated Press, A/P; page 32, Judi
Bottoni, Associated Press, A/P; page 38, Peter Kramer, Getty Images; page 40,
Michael Montes, WireImage.com/AI Wire Photo Service

Printed in the United States of America.

1 2 3 4 5 6 11 10 09 08 07 06 05

Table of Contents

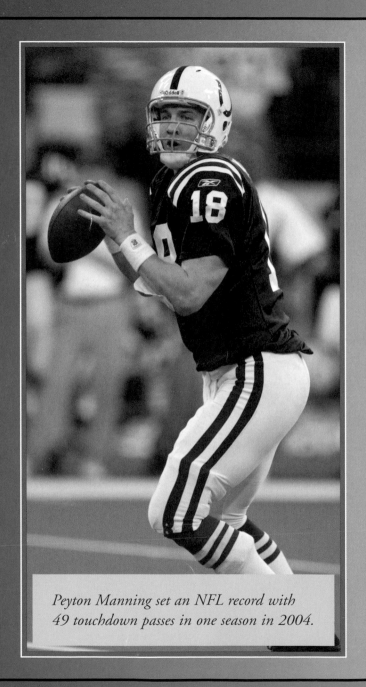

Peyton Manning set an NFL record with 49 touchdown passes in one season in 2004.

Chapter 1

Peyton Manning

The clock shows one minute to play in the game.
The Indianapolis Colts have the football.
They trail the San Diego Chargers by eight points.
Peyton Manning drops back to pass. He throws.
*Touchdown! Peyton Manning has the **NFL** record!*

A New Record

On December 26, 2004, Peyton Manning threw his 49th touchdown pass of the season. That broke Dan Marino's NFL record of 48. Marino had held the record for 20 years.

But Peyton didn't stop to enjoy the record. The game wasn't over, so Peyton played on. His team won 34–31 in **overtime**.

NFL: short for *National Football League*
overtime (OH-vur-time): an extra period of play added to a game that is tied

Proud Parents

Peyton's parents saw him set the record.
His dad, Archie, was also a great **quarterback**.
Archie said touchdown passes are great, but a
quarterback remembers something else more.
"You'll always remember your **comeback wins**,"
Archie said. "It was a very special day."

quarterback (KWOR-tur-bak): the player who leads the
offense in football
comeback win (KUHM-bak WIN): when you are losing
a game, but end up winning

Archie Manning (right) greets his son Peyton. Peyton had just set an NFL record for touchdown passes in one season.

Growing Up

Peyton was born on March 24, 1976. He grew up in New Orleans with his two brothers. All three boys loved sports. In high school, they played football, baseball, and basketball. Peyton liked football best.

Peyton played quarterback in high school. In three seasons, his team won 34 games. They lost only five. Peyton passed for 7,207 yards and 92 touchdowns. As a **senior**, Peyton won the Gatorade Circle of Champions National Player of the Year Award.

---

senior (SEE-nyur): a person in the fourth year of high school

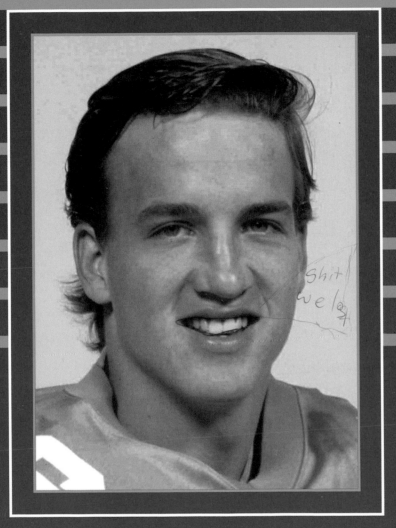

Peyton won a national player of the year award in high school.

Playing in College

Many colleges wanted Peyton to play football for them. Peyton's dad wanted him to go to the University of Mississippi. That's where Archie had gone to college. But Peyton chose the University of Tennessee.

At Tennessee, Peyton set 33 records. His teams won 39 games and lost only six. Peyton passed for 89 touchdowns and 11,201 yards. In 1997, he was **runner-up** for the Heisman Trophy. Each year, this award goes to the best college football player in the United States.

runner-up (RUHN-er-UHP): the person or team that comes in second in a contest

Peyton played quarterback at the University of Tennessee. Here he runs toward the end zone.

Playing in the NFL

Peyton **graduated** from college in 1998.
Now NFL football teams wanted him.
Each year, the NFL has a **draft** when
teams get to pick new players. In 1998,
the Indianapolis Colts got to choose first.
They picked Peyton.

Peyton turned out to be a good choice.
From 1998 through 2004, he passed
for 216 touchdowns and 29,442 yards.
In 2004, he was named the Most **Valuable**
Player in the NFL.

How Did He Get So Good?

Just how did Peyton get to be so good?
Where did he learn his quarterback skills?
Let's meet Peyton's family and find out.

---

graduate (GRAJ-oo-ate): to pass and finish all courses
in school
draft (DRAFT): a meeting where teams pick players for
their team
valuable (VAL-yoo-uh-buhl): very important in some way

As quarterback for the Indianapolis Colts, Peyton drops back to pass.

Archie Manning played quarterback for the New Orleans Saints from 1971 to 1981.

CHAPTER 2

Archie Manning

*He never won a **Super Bowl**.*

*He never won a college **championship**.*

Yet he was an All-America quarterback in college.

In the NFL, he won a player of the year award.

Who is he? He is Peyton Manning's father, Archie.

Early Years

Archibald Elisha Manning III was born on May 19, 1949. He grew up in Drew, Mississippi. His family had little money.

Archie played football, basketball, and baseball as a teenager. He liked baseball best. In seventh grade, Archie was already playing on the high school baseball team.

Super Bowl (SOO-pur BOHL): a final game to decide the best team in the NFL

championship (CHAM-pee-uhn-ship): a final game to decide the top player or team in a sport

Two-Sport Star

At first, Archie played running back in football. But in high school, his coach switched him to quarterback.

During high school, Archie was often hurt. He missed many games. Still, when he graduated, many colleges wanted him to play football for them.

Major League Baseball also wanted Archie. Archie could make money playing baseball. If he went to college, he could study and play football, but he wouldn't get paid. What would you do?

Archie was a star at both football and baseball.

College First

Archie decided to go to college. He chose the University of Mississippi. This college is also called "Ole Miss." Before long, Archie was the starting quarterback on the football team. But then something horrible happened.

Part of the campus at the University of Mississippi

The speed limit on the streets at Ole Miss is 18 miles per hour. Can you guess why?

Playing for the Saints

In 1971, the New Orleans Saints chose Archie to play on their NFL team. Archie played for the Saints for 11 years. In 1978, he was named **NFC** Player of the Year. Twice he played in the Pro Bowl with the very best NFL players.

The Saints were not a very good team, however. There was one bright side, though. Archie could take his sons to practices and games. Sometimes the boys even got to practice with the team.

Only Part of the Story

Archie and his son Peyton have won many awards. But that is just part of the Manning story. What else might there be to learn about this family?

NFC: short for *National Football Conference*

Archie played 11 years for the New Orleans Saints. He also played for the Houston Oilers and the Minnesota Vikings.

Eli Manning also played quarterback for Ole Miss.

CHAPTER 3

Eli Manning

In 2001, Ole Miss played the University of Arkansas.
The game went into a total of seven overtimes!
The Ole Miss quarterback passed for 312 yards and
six touchdowns. But Arkansas still won, 58–56.

A Family Game

Does this story sound familiar to you?
The word *familiar* comes from *family*.
What does family have to do with football?
The Ole Miss quarterback that day came
from a famous football family.

His name? Elisha "Eli" Nelson Manning.
Eli is also Archie Manning's son!

Following the Family Footsteps

Eli Manning is Peyton's younger brother. As kids, they were different from each other. Peyton teased Eli a lot. Peyton was **intense** and **aggressive**. Eli was quieter and more easygoing. In fact, his nickname was "Easy."

Eli went to the same high school as Peyton. There Eli threw for 7,389 yards. That was 182 yards more than Peyton. Eli had 81 touchdowns. Peyton had 92.

intense (in-TENSS): showing strong feelings
aggressive (uh-GRES-iv): bold and active

Peyton, Archie, and Eli pose for a family photo.

Just Like Dad

After high school, Eli went to Ole Miss like his dad. Eli also played quarterback.

Like his dad and brother, Eli played great football at college. He passed for 10,119 yards and 81 touchdowns. Eli now has 47 school records at Ole Miss.

Ready for the NFL

In 2004, the San Diego Chargers made Eli the first pick in the NFL draft. The Chargers then **traded** him to the New York Giants.

In his first year, Eli played in nine games for the Giants. He started seven of those games. He passed for 1,043 yards and six touchdowns.

---

trade (TRADE): to give up a player in return for another player or players

Eli Manning playing quarterback for the New York Giants

Another Great

You have read about three great football players in the Manning family. But there is one more Manning brother—Cooper. Why do you think Cooper is not as well-known as his father and brothers?

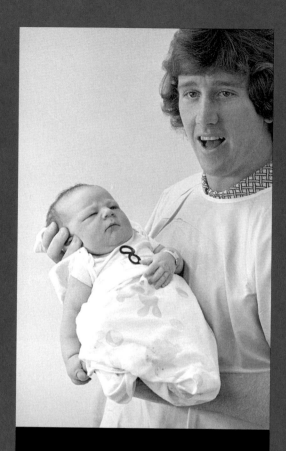

Archie holds his first-born son, Cooper. Cooper later wore number "8" and took after his dad in many ways.

— CHAPTER 4 —

Cooper Manning

Cooper Manning was a high school football star, too.
*Unlike Peyton and Eli, Cooper played **wide receiver**.*
In 1990, his quarterback was little brother Peyton!
You can almost hear youngest brother Eli in the stands,
shouting, "It's Manning to Manning—touchdown!"

Brothers

Cooper Manning liked to pick fights with his brothers. He most often picked fights with Peyton. Archie told his three sons how lucky they were to have each other. Of course, they didn't listen. They were too busy **competing**. Each son wanted to beat the other.

---

wide receiver (WIDE ri-SEE-vur): a football player whose main job is to catch passes thrown by the quarterback
compete (kuhm-PEET): to try hard to do better than others at a task or contest

Waiting to Play

In high school, Cooper also hoped to play quarterback. But two other quarterbacks were ahead of him. For two years, he waited. Then, Cooper became a wide receiver instead.

The Manning family runs a camp to train young quarterbacks. Here, some campers do drills, just as brothers Cooper, Peyton, and Eli did when they were boys.

Bad News

Cooper's hand didn't get better. It was still numb. Sometimes it hurt. He went to another doctor. This time the news was worse. Cooper hadn't hurt his hand playing football, the doctor said. Cooper had been born with a problem in his **spine**.

Cooper had to have **surgery** right away to fix his spine. He also had to quit playing football—forever! The doctor said that Cooper was lucky. He said Cooper could have been **paralyzed** from playing football.

The news was very hard on Cooper. But over time, he got used to it. Later he said, "I guess I played my **career** a hit away from the wheelchair."

spine (SPINE): a person's or animal's backbone
surgery (SUR-jer-ee): the act of cutting open someone's body to repair a damaged or diseased part
paralyze (PAR-uh-lize): to become unable to move
career (kuh-RIHR): the work that a person does

Starting Over

After Cooper's surgery, he couldn't walk. His right leg was **useless**. His left leg was numb. It took months for him to get his strength back and learn to walk again.

Cooper had to give up college football. His dream of playing in the NFL was over. But he did go back to Ole Miss and graduate. Today, he is a **successful** businessman in New Orleans.

---

useless (YOOSS-liss): not able to work at all
successful (suhk-SESS-fuhl): turning out well

Special Family

The Mannings are a special family. What do you think makes them a success in sports and in business? What makes them a success as a family?

Peyton and Eli Manning are two of the NFL's superstars.

CHAPTER 5

Family

Each of the Manning boys was a great athlete.

Today, two play in the National Football League.

Did their parents push them to be superstars?

How to Raise a Quarterback

Archie has this to say about raising kids.
"The key is, don't try to raise a quarterback.
Because I didn't try to raise a quarterback.
I tried to just be there for my children and
tried to get them through their **adolescence**
in good shape."

---

adolescence (ad-uh-LESS-uhns): the time of life between
childhood and adulthood

Archie enjoys spending time with his sons.
Here he is with Peyton and Eli.

Proud Dad

Archie and his wife, Olivia, knew that each of their boys was different. They didn't try to make them into athletes. They let them find sports for themselves. Dad and Mom were there to help them—but only when the boys asked.

Archie feels **fortunate** to have been so successful in football. He and Olivia are also very proud of each of their sons. They enjoy watching them play sports and grow to be young men.

Archie said he only wishes his own dad could be there watching, too.

"I could have taken him along on so many things," Archie said. "I think he would have enjoyed it. I think he would have been proud."

---

fortunate (FOR-chuh-nit): lucky; blessed

Epilogue

Manning Family Facts

Archie Manning (born 1949)

President of his high school senior class

Lettered in four high school sports

Valedictorian of his high school senior class

Chosen 1978 NFC Player of the Year

Cooper Manning (born 1974)

Ran the 40-yard dash in 4.7 seconds in
high school

Won a high school state basketball championship

Named Most Valuable Player for his high school
football team

Two-time all-state high school football player

---

letter (LET-ur): to win an award for playing a varsity sport
valedictorian (va-luh-dik-TOR-ee-uhn): a student who
speaks at graduation; usually the one with the highest grades

Peyton Manning (born 1976)

Received the NCAA (National Collegiate Athletic Association) Today's Top VIII Award for outstanding achievement in athletics, academics, and community services

Graduated from college with honors and a 3.6 GPA

Started the PeyBack Foundation in 1999 to help needy youth

Eli Manning (born 1981)

Lettered in three high school sports

Wore the same undershirt during games in high school and college that Peyton and Cooper wore

Named to the 2000, 2001, and 2002 SEC (Southeast Conference) **Academic Honor Roll**

Received the NCAA Today's Top VIII Award

academic honor role (ak-uh-DEM-ik ON-ur ROHL): an award given to athletes who have a grade point of 3.0 or higher

Glossary

academic honor role (ak-uh-DEM-ik ON-ur ROHL): an award given to athletes who have a grade point of 3.0 or higher

adolescence (ad-uh-LESS-uhns): the time of life between childhood and adulthood

aggressive (uh-GRES-iv): bold and active

career (kuh-RIHR): the work that a person does

championship (CHAM-pee-uhn-ship): a final game to decide the top player or team in a sport

comeback win (KUHM-bak WIN): when you are losing a game but end up winning

compete (kuhm-PEET): to try hard to do better than others at a task or contest

draft (DRAFT): a meeting where teams pick players for their team

drill (DRILL): an activity done over and over to learn something

fortunate (FOR-chuh-nit): lucky; blessed

graduate (GRAJ-oo-ate): to pass and finish all courses in school

intense (in-TENSS): showing strong feelings

junior (JOO-nyur): a person in the third year of high school

letter (LET-ur): to win an award for playing a varsity sport

NFL: short for *National Football League*

numb (NUHM): unable to feel anything

operate (OP-uh-rate): to cut open someone's body to repair a hurt or diseased part

overtime (OH-vur-time): an extra period of play added to a game that is tied

paralyze (PAR-uh-lize): to become unable to move

quarterback (KWOR-tur-bak): the player who leads the offense in football

retire (ri-TIRE): to put aside and honor by not letting others wear that number on their jersey

runner-up (RUHN-er-UHP): the person or team that comes in second in a contest

senior (SEE-nyur): a person in the fourth year of high school

spine (SPINE): a person's or animal's backbone

successful (suhk-SESS-fuhl): turning out well

Super Bowl (SOO-pur BOHL): a final game to decide the best team in the NFL

surgery (SUR-jer-ee): the act of cutting open someone's body to repair a hurt or diseased part

trade (TRADE): to give up a player in return for another player or players

tragedy (TRA-juh-dee): a very sad event

useless (YOOSS-liss): not able to work at all

valedictorian (val-uh-dik-TOR-ee-uhn): a student who speaks at graduation; usually the one with the highest grades

valuable (VAL-yoo-uh-buhl): very important in some way
wide receiver (WIDE ri-SEE-vur): a football player whose main job is to catch passes thrown by the quarterback

Bibliography

Buckley, James Jr. *Peyton Manning.* Dorling Kindersley Readers. New York: Dorling Kindersley, 2001.

Frisaro, Joe. *Peyton Manning: Passing Legacy.* Football Superstar Series (3). Champaign, Ill.: Sports Publishing, 1999.

Rappoport, Ken. *Super Sports Star Peyton Manning.* Super Sports Star. Berkeley Heights, N.J.: Enslow Publishers, 2003.

Savage, Jeff. *Peyton Manning.* Amazing Athletes. Minneapolis: LernerSports, 2004.

Stewart, Mark. *Peyton Manning: Rising Son.* Football's New Wave. Brookfield, Conn.: Millbrook Press, 2000.

Useful Addresses

National Football League
280 Park Avenue
New York, NY 10017

Internet Sites

Indianapolis Colts
http://www.colts.com

New Orleans Saints
http://www.neworleanssaints.com

New York Giants
http://www.giants.com

NFL.com
http://www.nfl.com

Peyton Manning
http://www.peytonmanning.com

Index